The Poetry of Dora Sigerson Shorter

Volume II - The Fairy Changeling & Other Poems

Dora Mary Sigerson was born in Dublin on August 16th, 1866, the daughter of George Sigerson, a surgeon and writer, and Hester (née Varian) also a writer.

Her father was a leader in Dublin's intellectual world and immersed the young Dora in the vibrant literary society of Dublin throughout her childhood, helping her gain a deep and complete love of her country. Like her father, Dora was active in the Irish literary revival, and a passionate campaigner for home rule.

Her poetry collections date from 1893 and are particularly evocative when she writes of her homeland, War and, most of all, the Easter Rising of 1916. Her friends included Katharine Tynan, the noted Irish poet and author as well as fellow writers and poets Rose Kavanagh and Alice Furlong

When she married Clement King Shorter, an English journalist and literary critic, in 1895 they moved to England and she wrote under the name Dora Sigerson Shorter. Although in England her heart's passion remained with Ireland.

The tragic events of Easter 1916, were a terrible blow to her and her health quickly began to fail.

Dora Mary Sigerson Shorter died on January 6th, 1918. The cause of her death was not disclosed.

As well as a foremost poet Dora's talents extended to sculpture, journalism and novels.

Dora's best-known sculpture is the memorial in Glasnevin Cemetery to the executed leaders of the Easter Rebellion.

In her lifetime she was renowned for her personal beauty and her charm. That charm is reflected in her works which are full of eagerness, love, sympathy, and, of course, suffering.

Index of Contents

DORA SIGERSON - A TRIBUTE AND SOME MEMORIES by Katharine Tynan

To think of Dora Sigerson—and it is a poignant thought—takes one back to Dublin in the 'nineties, or the later 'eighties. I think it was on a summer Sunday in 1887 that Dr. Sigerson came to see me with his two daughters and Rose Kavanagh, whom I already knew. The Yeatses were there that Sunday for the big meal at a most unfashionable hour, which was a feature of those years for the young writers and artists of Dublin. My old home was in the country, just under the Dublin mountains, and, I think, a very delightful place.

Everyone, of course, knew Dr. Sigerson by repute. The house was full of the young that day, with just a sprinkling of the young of heart like Mr. Yeats and my father and Dr. Sigerson. I remember that my brother said to me, "Miss Sigerson is very beautiful." She was. Her face then had some curious suggestion of the Greek Hermes. She wore her dark hair short, and it was in heavy masses. She had a beautiful brow and eyebrows, very fine grey eyes, a short straight nose, a warm pale colour, and vivid red lips. A little later the Irish-American, Miss Louise Imogen Guiney, dedicated her "Roadside Harp" to the Sigerson sisters:

There in the Druid brake,
If the cuckoo be awake
Again, oh, take my rhyme,
And keep it long for the sake
Of a bygone primrose-time.
You of the star-bright head
That twilight thoughts sequester:
You to your native fountains led,
Like to a young Muse garlanded:
Dora, and Hester.

Dora was indeed "like to a young Muse garlanded." She was singularly beautiful, with some strange hint of storm in her young beauty. She was so full of artistic impulse and achievement of many kinds, and she arrived at so much of art without any apprenticeship that the word "genius" seems not inapplicable to her. Our friendship flowed straight on from that summer Sunday of 1887. Dr. Sigerson's house in Clare Street became my headquarters when I went into Dublin from my country home. Dora was always painting or writing or doing sculpture. I can remember her coming from somewhere downstairs to the drawing-room at No. 3, Clare Street, when I was announced, wearing a sort of sculptor's blouse. There is still in her old home, crowded with beautiful things, at least one head by her of a nymph or a dryad, strangely delicate and pensive.

I don't think she had read much poetry till John O'Leary, saying her poetry was too introspective, gave her Percy's "Reliques," whence the genesis of her fine ballad poetry. If she had any training as an art student for her painting and drawing and sculpture, it must have been very slight. The gifts came to her out of the air, so to speak; real gifts and nothing acquired.

For seven good years my life was inextricably interwoven with hers and Hester's. We had the same friends, the same merry-makings, the same tastes and aims. We were of the circle which revolved around the great old Fenian, John O'Leary, and his not less noble sister; we visited the American poets, Mr. and Mrs. Piatt, at Queenstown, where Mr. Piatt was American Consul; we spent many happy days at Mr. Richard Ashe King's delightful house at Waltham Terrace, Blackrock. We wrote for the same papers. Presently Dora Sigerson and I were together in politics, both Parnellites when the "split" came. Together we attended Mr. Parnell's meetings; we went to meet him when he returned to Dublin from the country; we lived through all the passionate loyalty of those days. Together we exulted; together we mourned; together we followed our chief to the grave, not thinking upon how she should one day lie near him.

Perhaps the best holiday we had together was a scamper through Donegal on some business about the industries for Lady Aberdeen. It was just before I was married. From the time we left Amiens Street Station till we returned it was all pure enjoyment. The people with their beautiful manners, the wonderful scenery, the hotels, the car-drivers, the priests, the little towns, the wild, lonely places, the great hospitality—all were a delight to her. She was full of the joie de vivre, despite the hint of tragedy in her beauty. She did madcap things. Like Martin Ross she could mimic animals perfectly. How we laughed when she crowed like a cock over a low wall beyond which was a poultry-yard, and the real Vizier, after one careful look around, marshalled all his ladies into an inner enclosure. I have somewhere a book of that tour with her delightfully humorous drawings. She was always pencil in hand. We did the whole of Donegal within a fortnight, and came back, blowzed but happy, I to my wedding, she to the Dublin she always loved. A year or two later she met Clement Shorter at our little house in Mount Avenue, Ealing.

One thing I must not omit to mention—her passionate love of animals. In the old, good days in Dublin she used to pick up waifs and strays of forlorn doghood and take them to the Dogs' Home. The boys in the street used to shout derision at us: "Go on! wid yer grand hats and ye to be starvin' yer dog!" The sense of humour supported us.

How we laughed and lived together! Ah, well:

Let nothing disturb thee,
Let nothing affright thee.
All passes,
Only God remaineth
For ever and ever.

I will not speak of her beautiful poetry, essential poetry, always with a passionate emotion to give it wings. It is for the critic. No one will say she was not happy in her English life, though her heart was always slipping away like a grey bird to Ireland. She had a very full life and she had absolute devotion and knew what a precious thing she had.

Her breakdown in health was sudden. She attributed it herself to her intense and isolated suffering—isolated beyond the perfect sympathy of her devoted husband—over the events following Easter week, 1916, in Dublin, and the troubles which menaced the country she adored. I think she need not have felt so bitterly isolated; the spirit of humanity is strong in the good English—and the good English are very good—but the fact remains that she broke her heart over it all; and so she died, as she would have chosen to die, for love of the Dark Rosaleen.

DORA SIGERSON by C. P. Curran

The finest side of Irish life and literature is poorer to-day by the death of Dora Sigerson. From her long residence in England she was known here mainly as a poet of a genius as distinguished as it was personal. But when, in recent years, affairs in Ireland grew more critical, her great-hearted personality emerged more clearly and shone the more brightly as the situation grew more dangerous. Love of Ireland was with her a passion. The events of Easter week moved her profoundly. She spent herself regally on behalf of her people with brain, pen and fortune and at the expense of her vitality. The best of the English weeklies said that "the rebellion killed her almost as surely as if she had stood with the rebels in O'Connell Street. Henceforth she could think of little else; of what had died with it and what might live." That is no less than the truth. She is fairly to be reckoned with the dead of Easter. Devotion to their cause consumed her like a flame into which she flung all her gifts, neither few nor negligible. She was a true artist, eagerly seeking expression for an ardent and manifold personality which itself transcended all her work, whether in poetry, sculpture or painting. Her poetry was saluted by the greatest contemporary names in England: Meredith, Francis Thompson, Swinburne, and the present writer has seen her name as the subject of lecture on the noticeboards of the Sorbonne. What faults lay on the surface of her verse were more than compensated for by its intensity, an intensity often tragic, "stoned by continual wreckage of her dreams," but always filled with pity. In the "Songs of the Irish Rebellion" and in her later work generally which we, in Ireland, will always consider her best, the passion that consumed her burnt away these superficial defects, themselves characteristic of her impetuous spirit. The poet of "Ireland," of the "Wind on the Hills," of "Ceann Dubh Dilis," of "Sixteen Dead Men," will always be remembered on that honourable roll of artists who, to the gain of both, fused with their art, the strong love of the people.

THE FAIRY CHANGELING

Dermod O'Byrne of Omah town
In his garden strode up and down;
He pulled his beard, and he beat his breast;
And this is his trouble and woe confessed:

"The good-folk came in the night, and they
Have stolen my bonny wean away;
Have put in his place a changeling,
A weashy, weakly, wizen thing!

"From the speckled hen nine eggs I stole,
And lighting a fire of a glowing coal,
I fried the shells, and I spilt the yolk;
But never a word the stranger spoke:

"A bar of metal I heated red
To frighten the fairy from its bed,
To put in the place of this fretting wean
My own bright beautiful boy again.

"But my wife had hidden it in her arms,
And cried 'For shame!' on my fairy charms;

She sobs, with the strange child on her breast:
'I love the weak, wee babe the best!'"

To Dermod O'Byrne's, the tale to hear,
The neighbours came from far and near:
Outside his gate, in the long boreen,
They crossed themselves, and said between

Their muttered prayers, "He has no luck!
For sure the woman is fairy-struck,
To leave her child a fairy guest,
And love the weak, wee wean the best!"

A BALLAD OF MARJORIE

"What ails you that you look so pale,
O fisher of the sea?"
"'Tis for a mournful tale I own,
Fair maiden Marjorie."

"What is the dreary tale to tell,
O toiler of the sea?"
"I cast my net into the waves,
Sweet maiden Marjorie.

"I cast my net into the tide,
Before I made for home;
Too heavy for my hands to raise,
I drew it through the foam."

"What saw you that you look so pale,
Sad searcher of the sea?"
"A dead man's body from the deep
My haul had brought to me!"

"And was he young, and was he fair?"
"Oh, cruel to behold!
In his white face the joy of life
Not yet was grown a-cold."

"Oh, pale you are, and full of prayer
For one who sails the sea."
"Because the dead looked up and spoke,
Poor maiden Marjorie."

"What said he, that you seem so sad,

O fisher of the sea?
(Alack! I know it was my love,
Who fain would speak to me!)"

"He said, 'Beware a woman's mouth—
A rose that bears a thorn.'"
"Ah, me! these lips shall smile no more
That gave my lover scorn."

"He said, 'Beware a woman's eyes.
They pierce you with their death.'"
"Then falling tears shall make them blind
That robbed my dear of breath."

"He said, 'Beware a woman's hair—
A serpent's coil of gold.'"
"Then will I shear the cruel locks
That crushed him in their fold."

"He said, 'Beware a woman's heart
As you would shun the reef.'"
"So let it break within my breast,
And perish of my grief."

"He raised his hands; a woman's name
Thrice bitterly he cried:
My net had parted with the strain;
He vanished in the tide."

"A woman's name! What name but mine,
O fisher of the sea?"
"A woman's name, but not your name,
Poor maiden Marjorie."

THE PRIEST'S BROTHER

Thrice in the night the priest arose
From broken sleep to kneel and pray.
"Hush, poor ghost, till the red cock crows,
And I a Mass for your soul may say."

Thrice he went to the chamber cold,
Where, stiff and still uncoffinèd,
His brother lay, his beads he told,
And "Rest, poor spirit, rest," he said.

Thrice lay the old priest down to sleep
Before the morning bell should toll;
But still he heard—and woke to weep—
The crying of his brother's soul.

All through the dark, till dawn was pale,
The priest tossed in his misery,
With muffled ears to hide the wail,
The voice of that ghost's agony.

At last the red cock flaps his wings
To trumpet of a day new-born.
The lark, awaking, soaring sings
Into the bosom of the morn.

The priest before the altar stands,
He hears the spirit call for peace;
He beats his breast with shaking hands.
"O Father, grant this soul's release.

"Most Just and Merciful, set free
From Purgatory's awful night
This sinner's soul, to fly to Thee,
And rest for ever in Thy sight."

The Mass is over—still the clerk
Kneels pallid in the morning glow.
He said, "From evils of the dark
Oh, bless me, father, ere you go.

"Benediction, that I may rest,
For all night did the Banshee weep."
The priest raised up his hands and blest—
"Go now, my child, and you will sleep."

The priest went down the vestry stair,
He laid his vestments in their place,
And turned—a pale ghost met him there,
With beads of pain upon his face.

"Brother," he said, "you have gained me peace,
But why so long did you know my tears,
And say no Mass for my soul's release,
To save the torture of all those years?"

"God rest you, brother," the good priest said,
"No years have passed—but a single night."
He showed the body uncoffinèd,

And the six wax candles still alight.

The living flowers on the dead man's breast
Blew out a perfume sweet and strong.
The spirit paused ere he passed to rest—
"God save your soul from a night so long."

Who knocks at the Geraldine's door to-night
In the black storm and the rain?
With the thunder crash and the shrieking wind
Comes the moan of a creature's pain.

And once they knocked, yet never a stir
To show that the Geraldine knew;
And twice they knocked, yet never a bolt
The listening Geraldine drew.

And thrice they knocked ere he moved his chair,
And said, "Whoever it be,
I dare not open the door to-night
For a fear that has come to me."

Three times he rises from out his chair,
And three times he sits him down.
"Now what has made faint this heart of mine?"
He says with a growing frown.

"Now what has made me a coward to-night,
Who never knew fear before?
But I swear that the hand of a little child
Keeps pulling me from the door."

The Geraldine rose from his chair at last
And opened the door full wide;
"Whoever is out in the storm," said he,
"May in God's name come inside!"

He who was out in the storm and rain
Drew back at the Geraldine's call.
"Now who comes not in the Holy Name
Will never come in at all."

He looked to the right, he looked to the left,
And never a one saw he;

But right in his path lay a coal black hound,
A-moaning right piteously.

"Come in," he cried, "you little black hound,
Come in, I will ease your pain;
My roof shall keep you to-night at least
From the leash of wind and rain."

The Geraldine took up the little black hound,
And put him down by the fire.
"So sleep you there, poor wandering one,
As long as your heart desire."

The Geraldine tossed on his bed that night,
And never asleep went he
For the crowing of his little red cock,
That did crow most woefully.

For the howling of his own wolf-hound,
That cried at the gate all night.
He rose and went to the banquet hall
At the first of morning light.

He looked to the right, he looked to the left,
At the rug where the dog lay on;
But the reindeer skin was burnt in two,
And the little black hound was gone.

And, traced in the ashes, these words he read:
"For the soul of your firstborn son,
I will make you rich as you once were rich
Ere the glass of your luck was run."

The Geraldine went to the west window,
And then he went to the east,
And saw his desolate pasture fields,
And the stables without a beast.

"So be it, as I love no woman,
No son shall ever be mine;
I would that my stables were full of steeds,
And my cellars were full of wine."

"I swear it, as I love no woman,
And never a son have I,
I would that my sheep and their little lambs
Should flourish and multiply.

"So yours be the soul of my firstborn son."
Here the Geraldine slyly smiled,
But from the dark of the lonely room
Came the cry of a little child.

The Geraldine went to the west window,
He opened, and out did lean,
And lo! the pastures were full of kine,
All chewing the grass so green.

And quickly he went to the east window,
And his face was pale to see,
For lo! he saw to the empty stalls
Brave steeds go three by three.

The Geraldine went to the great hall door,
In wonder at what had been,
And there he saw the prettiest maid
That ever his eyes had seen.

And long he looked at the pretty young maid,
And swore there was none so fair;
And his heart went out of him like a hound,
And hers like a timid hare.

Each day he followed her up and down,
And each night he could not rest,
Until at last the pretty young maid
Her love for him confessed.

They wooed and they wed, and the days went by
As quick as such good days will,
And at last came the cry of his firstborn son
The cup of his joy to fill.

And the summer passed, and the winter came;
Right fair was the child to see,
And he laughed at the shriek of a bitter storm
As he sat on his father's knee.

Who rings so loud at the Geraldine's gate?
Who knocks so loud at the door?
"Now rise you up, my pretty young wife,
For twice they have knocked before."

Quickly she opened the great hall door,
And "Welcome you in," she cried,
But there only entered a little black hound,

And he would not be denied.

When the Geraldine saw the little black dog,
He rose with a fearful cry,
"I sold my child to the Devil's hound
In forgotten days gone by."

He drew his sword on the little black hound,
But it would not pierce its skin,
He tried to pray, but his lips were dumb
Because of his grievous sin.

Then the fair young wife took the black hound's throat
Both her small white hands between.
And he thought he saw one of God's angels
Where his sweet young wife had been.

Then he thought he saw from God's spirit
The hound go sore oppressed,
But he woke to find his own dead wife
With her dead child on her breast.

Quickly he went to the west window,
Quickly he went to the east;
No help in the desolate pasture fields,
Or the stables that held no beast.

He flung himself at his white wife's side,
And the dead lips moved and smiled,
Then came somewhere from the lonely room
The laugh of a little child.

THE RAPE OF THE BARON'S WINE

Who was stealing the Baron's wine,
Golden sherry and port so old,
Precious, I wot, as drops of gold?
Lone to-night he came to dine,

Flung himself in his oaken chair,
Kicked the hound that whined for bread;
"God! the thief shall swing!" he said,
Thrust his hand through his ruffled hair.

Bolt and bar and double chain
Held secure the cellar door;

And the watchman placed before,
Kept a faithful watch in vain.

Every day the story came,
"Master, come! I hear it drip!"
The wine is wet on the robber's lip,
Who the robber, none could name.

All the folk in County Clare
Found a task for every day
By the Baron's gate to stray,
Came to gossip, stayed to stare.

Nothing here to satisfy
Souls for tragedy awake;
Just the castle by the lake,
Calmest spot beneath the sky.

But the whispered story grew,
When the Baron went to dine,
That a devil shared his wine,
Had his soul in danger too.

Every morn the Baron rose
More morose and full of age;
Passed the day in sullen rage,
Barred his gates on friends or foes.

Lone to-night he came to dine,
Struck the hound that asked a share,
Heard a step upon the stair—
"Come, the thief is at your wine!"

Baron of Killowen keep
Running down the vaulted way,
To the cellar dark by day,
Took the ten steps at a leap.

There he listened with the throng
Of frighted servants at the door,
He heard the wine drip on the floor,
And sea-mew's laughter loud and long.

Of oaken beam, of bolt and chain
They freed the door, and crowded through,
Their eyes a horror claimed in vain,
Nor ghost nor devil met their view.

They searched behind the hogshead, where
The watchful spider spied and span;
They sighed to see the wine that ran
A crimson torrent, wasting there.

They even searched the gloomy well
That legend said rose from the lake;
They saw bright bubbles rise and break,
But nothing stranger here befell.

The Baron cursed—the Baron said,
"Now all be gone, alone I'll stay,
There shall not rise another day
Without this thief, alive or dead."

So still he stood, no sound was there,
But just the wine went drop and drip;
Save that, the silence seemed to slip
Its threatening fingers through his hair.

And then as last an echo flew,
The splash of waters thrown apart;
He cursed the beating of his heart
Because the thief was listening too.

The slipping scrape of scales he hears,
And sea-mew laughter, loud and sweet;
He dares not move his frightened feet,
His pulse beats with a thousand fears.

At that strange monster in the gloom
He points his pistol quick, and fires;
Before the powder spark expires
He hears a sea-bird's scream of doom.

He saw one gleam of foam-white arms,
Of sea-green eyes, of sloak brown hair;
He had a glance to find her fair,
When he had slain her thousand charms.

The Baron of Killowen slew
A strange sea-maiden, young and fair;
And all the folk in county Clare
Will tell you that the tale is true.

And when the Baron came to dine,
His guests could never understand,
That he should say, with glass in hand,

"I would the thief were at my wine!"

CEAN DUV DEELISH

Cean duv deelish, beside the sea
I stand and stretch my hands to thee
Across the world.
The riderless horses race to shore
With thundering hoofs and shuddering, hoar,
Blown manes uncurled.

Cean duv deelish, I cry to thee
Beyond the world, beneath the sea,
Thou being dead.
Where hast thou hidden from the beat
Of crushing hoofs and tearing feet
Thy dear black head?

Cean duv deelish, 'tis hard to pray
With breaking heart from day to day,
And no reply;
When the passionate challenge of sky is cast
In the teeth of the sea and an angry blast
Goes by.

God bless the woman, whoever she be,
From the tossing waves will recover thee
And lashing wind.
Who will take thee out of the wind and storm,
Dry thy wet face on her bosom warm
And lips so kind?

I not to know. It is hard to pray,
But I shall for this woman from day to day,
"Comfort my dead,
The sport of the winds and the play of the sea."
I loved thee too well for this thing to be,
O dear black head!

BANAGHER RHUE

Banagher Rhue of Donegal,
(Holy Mary, how slow the dawn!)
This is the hour of your loss or gain:

Is go d-tigheadh do, mhûirnín slan! {*}

Banagher Rhue, but the hour was ill
(O Mary Mother, how high the price!)
When you swore you'd game with Death himself;
Aye, and win with the devil's dice.

Banagher Rhue, you must play with Death,
(Mary, watch with him till the light!)
Through the dark hours, for the words you said,
All this strange and noisy night.

Banagher Rhue, you are pale and cold;
(How the demons laugh through the air!)
The anguish beads on your frowning brow;
Mary set on your lips a prayer!

Banagher Rhue, you have won the toss:
(Mother, pray for his soul's release!)
Shuffle and deal ere the black cock crows,
That your spirit may find its peace.

Banagher Rhue, you have played a king;
(How strange a light on your fingers fall!)
A voice, "I was cold, and he sheltered me . . ."
The trick is gained, but your chance is small.

Banagher Rhue, now an ace is yours;
(Mother Mary, the night is long!)
"I was a sin that he hurried aside . . ."
O for the dawn and the blackbird's song!

Banagher Rhue, now a ten of suit;
(Mother Mary, what hot winds blow!)
"Nine little lives hath he saved in his path . . ."
And the black cock that does not crow.

Banagher Rhue, you have played a knave;
(O what strange gates on their hinges groan!)
"I was a friend who had wrought him ill;
When I had fallen he cast no stone . . ."

Banagher Rhue, now a queen has won!
(The black cock crows with the flash of dawn.)
And she is the woman who prays for you:
"Is go d-tigheadh do, mhûirnín slan!"

{*} *"May my darling come through safely!"*

THE FAIR LITTLE MAIDEN

"There is one at the door, Wolfe O'Driscoll,
At the door, who is bidding you come!"
"Who is he that wakes me in the darkness,
Calling when all the world's dumb?"

"Six horses has he to his carriage,
Six horses blacker than the night,
And their twelve red eyes in the shadows
Twelve lamps he carries for his light;

"And his coach is a coffin black and mouldy,
A huge black coffin open wide:
He asks for your soul, Wolfe O'Driscoll,
Who is calling at the door outside."

"Who let him thro' the gates of my gardens,
Where stronger bolts have never been?"
"'Twas the father of the fair little maiden
You drove to her grave so green."

"And who let him pass through the courtyard,
By loosening the bar and the chain?"
"Oh, who but the brother of the maiden,
Who lies in the cold and the rain!"

"Then who drew the bolts at the portal,
And into my house bade him go?"
"She, the mother of the poor young maiden,
Who lies in her youth so low."

"Who stands, that he dare not enter,
The door of my chamber, between?"
"O, the ghost of the fair little maiden,
Who lies in the churchyard green."

AT CHRISTMAS TIME

For that old love I once adored
I decked my halls and spread my board
At Christmas time.
With all the winter's flowers that grow

I wreathed my room, and mistletoe
Hung in the gloom of my doorway,
Wherein my dear lost love might stray
When joy-bells chime.

What phantom was it entered there
And drank his wine and took his chair
At Christmas time?
With holly boughs and mistletoe
He crowned his head, and at my woe
And tears I shed laughed long and loud;
"Get back, O phantom! to thy shroud
When joy-bells chime."

A WEEPING CUPID

Why love! I thought you were gay and fair,
Merry of mien and debonair.
What then means this brow so black,
Whose sullen gloom twin eyes give back,
Poor little god in tears, alack!

Why love! I thought in your smiling cheek
Dainty dimples played hide and seek;
Passing by like a winter's night,
With stormy sighs from lips all white.
Poor little god, how comes your plight?

A maiden said you were tall and bold,
With an arm of steel and a heart of gold;
Whose changing face would make her day;
When came a frown, the sunshine play
Of smiles would chase the clouds away.

A youth once said you were like a maid
With sunny hair in a golden braid;
Whose cheeks were each a rose uncurled;
And brow a lilybell unfurled;
The fairest maid in all the world.

Why love! I find you so weak and small,
A human child, not a god at all;
Two angry, sleepy eyes that cry,
Two little hands so soft and shy,
I'll hush you with a lullaby.
Come, love!

THE LOVER

I go through wet spring woods alone,
Through sweet green woods with heart of stone,
My weary foot upon the grass
Falls heavy as I pass.
The cuckoo from the distance cries,
The lark a pilgrim in the skies;
But all the pleasant spring is drear.
I want you, dear!

I pass the summer meadows by,
The autumn poppies bloom and die;
I speak alone so bitterly
For no voice answers me.
"O lovers parting by the gate,
O robin singing to your mate,
Plead you well, for she will hear
'I love you, dear!'"

I crouch alone, unsatisfied,
Mourning by winter's fireside.
O Fate, what evil wind you blow.
Must this be so?
No southern breezes come to bless,
So conscious of their emptiness
My lonely arms I spread in woe,
I want you so.

A BIRD FROM THE WEST

At the grey dawn, amongst the felling leaves,
A little bird outside my window swung,
High on a topmost branch he trilled his song,
And "Ireland! Ireland! Ireland!" ever sung.

Take me, I cried, back to my island home;
Sweet bird, my soul shall ride between thy wings;
For my lone spirit wide his pinions spread,
And home and home and home he ever sings.

We lingered over Ulster stern and wild.
I called: "Arise! doth none remember me?"

One turnèd in the darkness murmuring,
"How loud upon the breakers sobs the sea!"

We rested over Connaught—whispering said:
"Awake, awake, and welcome! I am here."
One woke and shivered at the morning grey;
"The trees, I never heard them sigh so drear."

We flew low over Munster. Long I wept:
"You used to love me, love me once again!"
They spoke from out the shadows wondering;
"You'd think of tears, so bitter falls the rain."

Long over Leinster lingered we. "Good-bye!
My best beloved, good-bye for evermore."
Sleepless they tossed and whispered to the dawn;
"So sad a wind was never heard before."

Was it a dream I dreamt? For yet there swings
In the grey morn a bird upon the bough,
And "Ireland! Ireland! Ireland!" ever sings.
Oh! fair the breaking day in Ireland now.

ALL SOULS' EVE

I cried all night to you,
I called till day was here;
Perhaps you could not come,
Or were too tirèd, dear.

Your chair I set by mine,
I made the dim hearth glow,
I whispered, "When he comes
I shall not let him go."

I closed the shutters tight,
I feared the dawn of day,
I stopped the busy clock
That timed your hours away.

Loud howled my neighbour's dog,
O glad was I to hear.
The dead are going by,
Now you will come, my dear,

To take the chair by mine—

Until the cock would crow—
O, if it be you came
And could not let me know,

For once a shadow passed
Behind me in the room,
I thought your loving eyes
Would meet mine in the gloom.

And once I thought I heard
A footstep by my chair,
I raised my eager hands,
But no sweet ghost was there.

We were too wide apart—
You in your spirit land—
I knew not when you came,
I could not understand.

Your eyes perhaps met mine,
Reproached me through the gloom,
Alas, for me alone
The empty, empty room!

The dead were passing home,
The cock crew loud and clear,
Mavourneen, if you came,
I knew not you were here.

AN IMPERFECT REVOLUTION

They crowded weeping from the teacher's house,
Crying aloud their fear at what he taught,
Old men and young men, wives and maids unwed,
And children screaming in the crowds unsought:
Some to their temples with accustomed feet
Bent—as the oxen go beneath the rod,
To fling themselves before some pictured saint,
"Alas! God help us if there is no God."

Some to the bed-side of their dying kind
To clasp with arms afraid to loose their hold;
Some to a church-yard falling on a grave
To kiss the carven name with lips as cold.
Some watched from break of day into the night.
The flash of birds, the bloom of flower and tree,

The whirling worlds that glimmer in the dark,
All said: "God help us if no God there be."

Some hid in caves and chattered mad with fear
At the uprising of the patient poor.
"He suffers with you," no more could they say,
Thus lock with keys of Heaven their bonds secure,
Some called their dead, and then remembering fell
Abusing death and cursed the wormy grave,
And wept for their long hoped-for Paradise,
"God help us if there be no God to save!"

And others sought for right and found it not,
And, seeking duty, found that it was dead,
Blamed their long blameless lives and vowed no more
To sacrifice, for "Might is right" they said.
And pleasure, leaping in the streets with sin,
Caroused through many days till wearily
She tired and met with death in bitter pain.
"Alas! God help us if no God we gain."

A few rose up and speaking, "O be strong,"
Were answered, "There's no reason for your right,"
But many crept in thankfulness for rest
Into the river's darkness out of sight;
And others with their limbs deformed, or sore
Seared flesh, shrieked out their patient years of pain.
Crying to Death for their lost plains of Heaven.
"Alas! God help us if no God we gain."

LOVE

Deep in the moving depths
Of yellow wine,
I swore I'd drown your face,
O love of mine;
All clad in yellow hue,
So fair to see,
You crouched within my cup
And laughed at me.

Twice o'er a learned page
I turned and tossed,
For would I not forget
The love I lost.
All stern and robed in gloom,

You read it too,
I could not see the words—
Saw only you.

Within the hungry chase
I thought to kill
You, love, who haunted thus
Without my will,
But in the gentle gaze
Of fawn and deer,
Your eyes disarmed my hand,
And shook my spear.

Beneath a maid's dark lash
I swore you'd drown,
Sink in the laughing blue—
Give in, go down:
But no! you bathèd there
Right joyously,
And from her liquid eyes
You laughed at me.

WISHES

I wish we could live as the flowers live,
To breathe and to bloom in the summer and sun;
To slumber and sway in the heart of the night,
And to die when our glory had done.

I wish we could love as the bees love,
To rest or to roam without sorrow or sigh;
With laughter, when, after the wooer had won,
Love flew with a whispered good-bye.

I wish we could die as the birds die,
To fly and to fall when our beauty was best:
No trammels of time on the years of our face;
And to leave but an empty nest.

CUPID SLAIN

I come from a burial;
Hush! let me be:
I have put away my love,

Fair exceedingly.

Ah! the little gold curls
Soft about his face;
Now my heart is sorrowful
For his sleeping-place.

But he would pursue me,
Never let me rest;
Till I turned and slew him,
Knowing it were best.

Laid his bow beside him,
Shovelled in the clay;
To-morrow I'll forget him;
Let me weep to-day.

WHAT WILL YOU GIVE?

What will you give me, if I will wed?
"A golden gown
To come sweetly down,
And deck you from foot to head."

How will you keep me, if I am cold?
"By a heart so warm,
The bravest storm
Dare not force through my strong hands' hold."

How will you please me, if I should thirst?
"Why by the rape
Of the purple grape,
Which the summer and sun have nursed."

If I should hunger what may I eat?
"For you the skies
The falcon flies,
And the hounds on the stag are fleet."

How can you comfort when fair youth dies,
When the spirit's fain
For a purer gain,
Than the satisfied flesh supplies?

"But this I promise, when starved and cold
A lonely soul

Finds for its goal
A six-foot bed and churchyard mould."

A MEADOW TRAGEDY

Here's a meadow full of sunshine
Ripe grasses lush and high;
There's a reaper on the roadway,
And a lark hangs in the sky.

There's a nest of love enclosing
Three little beaks that cry;
The reapers in the meadow
And a lark hangs in the sky.

Here's a mead all full of summer,
And tragedy goes by
With a knife amongst the grasses,
And a song up in the sky.

AN ECLIPSE

Let there be an end
And all be done;
Pass over, fair eclipse,
That hides the sun.

Dear face that shades the light
And shadows me,
Begone, and give me peace,
And set me free.

THE SCALLOP SHELL

A scallop shell, loosed by the lifting tide,
Had left a friendly shore, the seas to brave;
Its lips of pink and snowy hollow shone
Pure in the sun, a pearl upon the wave.

It gleamed and passed—you burdened it with love,
With sweet long futures, new and dreamy days:
And named for me—because I held your hopes.

I bid you hush—not meriting your praise.

I pointed, where your vessel came to shore,
Wrecked where the tiny breakers rose and fell;
And bid your voyagers not put to sea
So fail a craft as this poor scallop shell.

WITH A ROSE

In the heart of a rose
Lies the heart of a maid;
If you be not afraid
You will wear it. Who knows?

In the pink of its bloom,
Lay your lips to her cheek;
Since a rose cannot speak,
And you gain the perfume.

If the dews on the leaf
Are the tears from her eyes;
If she withers and dies,
Why, you have the belief,

That a rose cannot speak,
Though the heart of a maid
In its bosom must fade,
And with fading must break.

FOR EVER

He heard it first upon the lips of love,
And loved it for love's sake;
A faithful word, that knows nor time nor change,
Nor lone heart-break.

It sung across his heart-strings like a breath
Of Heaven's faithfulness, that whispered "Never
To part, to lose, to linger from your gaze."
She said, "I love for ever."

He heard it then upon the lips of death,
Of things that fade and die;
A word of sorrow never to be stilled,

An ever echoing sigh.

And loneliness within his soul did dwell,
And struck upon his heart-strings, crying "Never
To meet, to have, to hold, to see again."
She said, "Good-bye for ever."

THE BLOW RETURNED

I struck you once, I do remember well.
Hard on the track of passion sorrow sped,
And swift repentance, weeping for the blow;
I struck you once—and now you're lying dead!

Now you are gone the blow no longer sleeps
In your forgiveness hushed through all the years;
But like a phantom haunts me through the dark,
To cry "You gave your own belovèd tears."

Stript now of all excuses, stern and stark,
With all your small transgressings dimmed or fled,
The ghost returns the blow upon my heart
I struck you once—and now you're lying dead.

VALE

Good-bye, sweet friend, good-bye,
And all the world must be
Between my friend and me;
And nothing is, dear heart,
But hands that meet to part;
Good-bye, sweet friend, good-bye.

Good-bye, sweet love, good-bye,
And one long grave must be
Between my love and me;
What comfort there, dear heart,
For hands that meet to part?
Good-bye, sweet love, good-bye.

THE SKELETON IN THE CUPBOARD

Just this one day in all the year
Let all be one, let all be dear;
Wife, husband, child in fond embrace,
And thrust the phantom from its place.
No bitter words, no frowning brow,
Disturb the Christmas festal, now
The skeleton's behind the door.

Nor let the child, with looks askance,
Find out its sad inheritance
From souls that held no happiness,
Of home, where love is seldom guest;
But in his coming years retain
This one sweet night that had no pain;
The skeleton's behind the door.

In vain you raise the wassail bowl,
And pledge your passion, soul to soul.
You hear the sweet bells ring in rhyme,
You wreath the room for Christmas time
In vain. The solemn silence falls,
The death watch ticks within the walls;
The skeleton taps on the door.

Then let him back into his place,
Let us sit out the old disgrace;
Nor seek the phantom now to lay,
That haunted us through every day;
For plainer is the ghost; useless
Is this pretence of happiness;
The skeleton taps on the door.

YOU WILL NOT COME AGAIN

The green has come to the leafless tree,
The earth brings forth its grain;
The flower has come for the honey bee:
You will not come again.

The birds have come to the empty nest,
All winter full of rain;
So music has come where the silence was:
You will not come again.

Love will come for the weak lambs' cry;
Alas for my heart's dull pain!

In the cycle of change I alone am lone:
You will not come again.

THE WRECKAGE

Love lit a beacon in thine eyes,
And I out in the storm,
And lo! the night had taken wings;
I dream me safe and warm.

Love lit a beacon in thine eyes,
A wreckers' light for me;
My heart is broken on the rocks;
I perish in the sea.

I AM THE WORLD

I am the song, that rests upon the cloud;
I am the sun:
I am the dawn, the day, the hiding shroud,
When dusk is done.

I am the changing colours of the tree;
The flower uncurled:
I am the melancholy of the sea;
I am the world.

The other souls that, passing in their place,
Each in their groove;
Out-stretching hands that chain me and embrace,
Speak and reprove.

"O atom of that law, by which the earth
Is poised and whirled;
Behold! you hurrying with the crowd assert
You are the world."

Am I not one with all the things that be
Warm in the sun?
All that my ears can hear, or eyes can see,
Till all be done.

Of song and shine, of changing leaf apart,
Of bud uncurled:

With all the senses pulsing at my heart,
I am the world.

One day the song that drifts upon the wind,
I shall not hear;
Nor shall the rosy shoots to eyes grown blind
Again appear.

Deaf, in the dark, I shall arise and throw
From off my soul,
The withered world with all its joy and woe,
That was my goal.

I shall arise, and like a shooting star
Slip from my place;
So lingering see the old world from afar
Revolve in space.

And know more things than all the wise may know
Till all be done;
Till One shall come who, breathing on the stars,
Blows out the sun.

A NEW YEAR

Behold! a new white world!
The falling snow
Has cloaked the last old year
And bid him go.

To-morrow! cries the oak-tree
To his heart,
My sealèd buds shall fling
Their leaves apart.

To-morrow! pipes the robin,
And again
How sweet the nest that long
Was full of rain.

To-morrow! bleats the sheep,
And one by one
My little lambs shall frolic
'Neath the sun.

For us, too, let some fair

To-morrow be,
O Thou who weavest threads
Of Destiny!

Thou wast a babe on that
Far Christmas Day,
Let us as children follow
In Thy way.

So that our hearts grown cold
'Neath time and pain,
With young sweet faith may blossom
Green again.

That empty promises
Of passing years
Spring into life, and not
Repenting tears.

So that our deeds upon
The earth may go,
As innocent as lambs,
And pure as snow.

THE KINE OF MY FATHER

The kine of my rather, they are straying from my keeping;
The young goat's at mischief, but little can I do:
For all through the night did I hear the Banshee keening;
O youth of my loving, and is it well with you?

All through the night sat my mother with my sorrow;
"Whisht, it is the wind, O one childeen of my heart!"
My hair with the wind, and my two hands clasped in anguish;
Black head of my darling! too long are we apart.

Were your grave at my feet, I would think it half a blessing;
I could herd then the cattle, and drive the goats away;
Many a Paternoster I would say for your safe keeping;
I could sleep above your heart, until the dawn of day.

I see you on the prairie, hot with thirst and faint with hunger;
The head that I love lying low upon the sand.
The vultures shriek impatient, and the coyote dogs are howling,
Till the blood is pulsing cold within your clenching hand.

I see you on the waters, so white, so still forlorn,
Your dear eyes unclosing beneath a foreign rain:
A plaything of the winds, you turn and drift unceasing,
No grave for your resting; O mine the bitter pain!

All through the night did I hear the Banshee keening:
Somewhere you are dying, and nothing can I do;
My hair with the wind, and my two hands clasped in anguish;
Bitter is your trouble—and I am far from you.

SANCTUARY

Neighbour! for pity a hound cries on your steps
With pleading eyes, with sore and weary feet.
Neighbour! your pity a poor beast doth implore;
Hunger and cold are busy in the street.
Then, neighbour! pause; 'tis no good work you do.
"Off from my door! I have no place for you."

Neighbour, your mercy! A heart of love is here,
Within this weary body—love is rare,
And seldom comes to cry before our door.
Then open wide, and take your little share.
Love pleads to be your servant, leal and true.
"Off from my step! I have no place for you."

From step to step abused, from door to door,
Whipped by the wind, and beaten by the rain,
With hunger at his throat, he passes on;
Yet one who follows shares the creature's pain.
One follows. Neighbour, stop! unless you rue.
"Off from my step! I have no place for you."

The gentle Christ had heard His crying hound,
And left His throne to track the weary feet.
He follows, though unseen, with bleeding heart,
Refused from door to door, from street to street.
Yes, one who follows had refusal too.
"Off from my door! I have no place for you."

AN EASTERN GOD

I saw an Eastern God to-day;
My comrades laughed; lest I betray

My secret thoughts, I mocked him too.
His many hands (he had no few,
This God of gifts and charity),
The marble race, that smiled on me,
I mocked, and said, "O God unthroned,
Lone exile from the faith you owned,
No priest to bring you sacrifice,
No censer with its breath of spice,
No land to mourn your funeral pyre.
O King, whose subjects felt your fire,
Now dead, now stone, without a slave,
Unfeared, unloved, you have no grave.
Poor God, who cannot understand,
And what of your fair Eastern land,
What dark brows brushed your dusky feet,
What warm hearts on your marble beat,
With many a prayer unanswered?"
My comrades laughed and passed. I said,
"If in those lands you wander still,
In spirit, God, and work your will,"
I whispered in the marble ear
So low—because the walls might hear—
The painted lips they smiled at me—
"O guard my love, where'er he be."

A FRIEND IN NEED

Who has room for a friend
Who has money to spend,
And a goblet of gold
For your fingers to hold,
At the wave of whose hand
Leap the salmon to land,
Drop the birds of the air,
Fall the stag and the hare.
Who has room for a friend
Who has money to lend?
We have room for a friend!

Who has room for a friend
Who has nothing to lend,
When the goblet of gold
Is as far from his hold
As the fleet-footed hare,
Or the birds of the air.
Who has room for a friend

Who has nothing to spend?
We know not such a friend.

IN A WOOD

Hush, 'tis thy voice!
No, but a bird upon the bough
Romancing to its mate, but where art thou
To bid my heart rejoice?

'Tis thy hand, speak!
No, but the branches striking in the wind
Let loose a withered leaf that falls behind
Blown to my cheek.

Hush, thy footfall!
No, 'tis a streamlet hidden in the fern,
Thus from dawn to dark I wait, I learn
Sorrow is all.

A VAGRANT HEART

O to be a woman! to be left to pique and pine,
When the winds are out and calling to this vagrant heart of mine.
Whisht! it whistles at the windows, and how can I be still?
There! the last leaves of the beech-tree go dancing down the hill.
All the boats at anchor they are plunging to be free—
O to be a sailor, and away across the sea!
When the sky is black with thunder, and the sea is white with foam,
The gray-gulls whirl up shrieking and seek their rocky home,
Low his boat is lying leeward, how she runs upon the gale,
As she rises with the billows, nor shakes her dripping sail.
There is danger on the waters—there is joy where dangers be—
Alas! to be a woman and the nomad's heart in me.

Ochone! to be a woman, only sighing on the shore—
With a soul that finds a passion for each long breaker's roar,
With a heart that beats as restless as all the winds that blow—
Thrust a cloth between her fingers, and tell her she must sew;
Must join in empty chatter, and calculate with straws—
For the weighing of our neighbour—for the sake of social laws.
O chatter, chatter, chatter, when to speak is misery,
When silence lies around your heart—and night is on the sea.
So tired of little fashions that are root of all our strife,

Of all the petty passions that upset the calm of life.
The law of God upon the land shines steady for all time;
The laws confused that man has made, have reason not nor rhyme.

O bird that fights the heavens, and is blown beyond the shore,
Would you leave your flight and danger for a cage to fight no more?
No more the cold of winter, or the hunger of the snow,
Nor the winds that blow you backward from the path you wish to go?
Would you leave your world of passion for a home that knows no riot?
Would I change my vagrant longings for a heart more full of quiet?
No!—for all its dangers, there is joy in danger too:
On, bird, and fight your tempests, and this nomad heart with you!

The seas that shake and thunder will close our mouths one day,
The storms that shriek and whistle will blow our breaths away.
The dust that flies and whitens will mark not where we trod.
What matters then our judging? we are face to face with God.

WHEN YOU ARE ON THE SEA

How can I laugh or dance as others do,
Or ply my rock or reel?
My heart will still return to dreams of you
Beside my spinning-wheel.

My little dog he cried out in the dark,
He would not whisht for me:
I took him to my side—why did he bark
When you were on the sea?

I fear the red cock—if he crow to-night—
I keep him close and warm,
'Twere ill with me, if he should wake in fright
And you out in the storm.

I dare not smile for fear my laugh would ring
Across your dying ears;
O, if you, drifting, drowned, should hear me sing
And think I had not tears.

I never thought the sea could wake such waves,
Nor that such winds could be;
I never wept when other eyes grew blind
For some one on the sea.

But now I fear and pray all things for you,

How many dangers be!
I set my wheel aside, what can I do
When you are on the sea?

MY NEIGHBOUR'S GARDEN

Why in my neighbour's garden
Are the flowers more sweet than mine?
I had never such bloom of roses,
Such yellow and pink woodbine.

Why in my neighbour's garden
Are the fruits all red and gold,
While here the grapes are bitter
That hang for my fingers' hold?

Why in my neighbour's garden
Do the birds all fly to sing?
Over the fence between us
One would think 'twas always spring.

I thought my own wide garden
Once more sweet and fair than all,
Till I saw the gold and crimson
Just over my neighbour's wall.

But now I want his thrushes,
And now I want his vine,
If I cannot have his cherries
That grow more red than mine.

The serpent 'neath his apples
Will tempt me to my fall,
And then—I'll steal my neighbour's fruit
Across the garden wall.

AN IRISH BLACKBIRD

This is my brave singer,
With his beak of gold;
Now my heart's a captive
In his song's sweet hold.

O, the lark's a rover,

Seeking fields above:
But my serenader
Hath a human love.

"Hark!" he says, "in winter
Nests are full of snow,
But a truce to wailing
Summer breezes blow."

"Hush!" he sings, "with night-time
Phantoms cease to be,
Join your serenader
Piping on his tree."

O, my little lover,
Warble in the blue;
Wingless must I envy
Skies so wide for you.

DEATH OF GORMLAITH

Gormlaith, wife of Niall Glendu,
Happy was your dream that night,
Dreamt you woke in sudden fright,
Niall of Ulster stood by you.

Niall of Ulster, dead and gone,
Many a year had come again,
Him who was in battle slain
Now your glad eyes rest upon.

Well your gaze caressed him o'er,
His dark head you loved so well,
Where the coulin curled and fell
On the clever brow he bore.

Those brave shoulders wide and strong,
Many a Dane had quaked to see,
Never a phantom fair as he,—
Wife of Glendu gazed so long.

Glad Queen Gormlaith, at the dawn
Up you sprang to draw him near,
Ah! the grey cock loud and clear
Crew, and then the Ghost was gone.

Stretched your arms in vain request,
Slipped and fell, and wounded sore
Called his name, then spake no more,
For the bed-stick pierced your breast.

Queen, your smiling lips were dumb
With that last dear name you cried,
Yet some had it, ere you died,
Niall of Ulster whispered, "Come."

UNKNOWN IDEAL

Whose is the voice that will not let me rest?
I hear it speak.
Where is the shore will gratify my quest,
Show what I seek?
Not yours, weak Muse, to mimic that far voice,
With halting tongue;
No peace, sweet land, to bid my heart rejoice
Your groves among.

Whose is the loveliness I know is by,
Yet cannot place?
Is it perfection of the sea or sky,
Or human face?
Not yours, my pencil, to delineate
The splendid smile!
Blind in the sun, we struggle on with Fate
That glows the while.

Whose are the feet that pass me, echoing
On unknown ways?
Whose are the lips that only part to sing
Through all my days?
Not yours, fond youth, to fill mine eager eyes
Or find that shore
That will not let me rest, nor satisfies
For evermore.

BEWARE

I closed my hands upon a moth
And when I drew my palms apart,
Instead of dusty, broken wings

I found a bleeding human heart.

I crushed my foot upon a worm
That had my garden for its goal,
But when I drew my foot aside
I found a dying human soul.

THE OLD MAID

She walks in a lonely garden
On the path her feet have made,
With high-heeled shoes, gold-buckled,
And gown of a flowered brocade;

The hair that falls on her shoulders,
Half-held with a ribbon tie,
Once glowed like the wheat in autumn,
Now grey as a winter sky.

Time on her brow with rough fingers
Writes his record of smiles and tears;
And her mind, like a golden timepiece,
He stopped in the long past years.

At the foot of the lonely garden,
When she comes to the trysting place
She knew of old, there she lingers,
With a blush on her withered face.

The children out on the common:
They climb to the garden wall;
And laugh: "He will come to-morrow!"
Who never will come at all.

And often over our sewing,
As I and my neighbour sit
To gossip over this story
That has never an end to it,

"He is dead," I would say, "that lover,
Who left her so long ago,"
But my neighbour would rest her needle
To answer, "He's false I know."

"For could it be he were sleeping.
With a love that was such as this

He'd have burst through the gates of silence,
And flown to meet her kiss."

Is she best with tears or laughter,
This dame in her old brocade?
My neighbour says she is holy,
With a faith that will not fade.

But the children out on the common
They answer her dreary call,
And say: "He will come to-morrow!"
Who never will come at all.

WIRASTRUA

Wirastrua, wirastrua, woe to me that you are dead!
The corpse has spoken from out his bed,
"Yesternight my burning brain
Throbbed and beat on the strings of pain:
Now I rest, all my dreaming's done,
In the world behind the sun.
Yesterday I toiled full sore,
To-day I ride in a coach and four.
Yesternight in the streets I lay,
To-night with kings, and as good as they."
Wirastrua! wirastrua! would I were lying as cold as you.

QUESTIONS

What is the secret of your life, browsing ox,
Ox the sweet grass eating?
Who strung the mighty sinews in your flesh?
Who set that great heart beating?

What is the secret of your death, soulless ox,
Ox so patiently waiting?
Why hath pain wove her net for your brain's anguish
If for you Death will gain no life's creating?

A LITTLE DOG

A little dog disturbed my trust in Heaven.

I praised most faithfully
All the great things that be,
Man's pain and pleasure even,
I said though hard this weighing
Of pains and tears and praying
He will reward most just.

I said your bitter weeping man or maid,
Your tears or laughter
Shall gain a just Hereafter;
Meet you the will of God then unafraid,
Gird you to your trials for God's abode
Is open for all sorrow;
Live for the great to-morrow.
There passed me on the road

A little dog with hungry eyes, and sad
Thin flesh all shivering,
All sore and quivering,
Whining beneath the fell disease he had.
I hurried home and praised God as before
For thus affording
To man rewarding,
The dog was whining outside my door.

I flung it wide, and said, Come enter in,
Outcast of God.
Beneath His rod
You suffer sore, poor beast, that had no sin.
Not at my door then must you cry complaining
Your lot unjust,
But His who thrust
You from His door your body maiming.

Not mine the pleasure that you bear this pain,
Hurled into being
Without hope of freeing
By grief and patience a soul for any gain.
Thus I reproached God while I tended
The sores to healing
A voice stealing
And whispering out of the beast I friended,

Said, "God had quickened my flesh, bestowing
Joys without measure,
Made for its pleasure,
An Eden's garden for ever glowing.
Gave me to Man, his care and protection

To gain and to give,
And bid us so live
In united bonds of help and affection.

"Man wrecked our garden, so we were hurled
Out from the skies
Of Paradise
Into the sorrows of a weeping world.
He forgets my care, I, as God has said,
Give still affection
For that connection
Which into all our bodies life has breathed.

"And why are you abusing God, and praising
With mock effacement
And false abasement
Your own heart's kindness, deeming it amazing
That you should do this duty for my sake,
Which is His bidding,
Nor blame for ridding
Himself of me, your neighbour, he who spake hard words,
Hard words and drove me forth all sore and ill?"

Thus while I tended
This dog I friended
Gave back my faith in Heaven by God's will.

"I PRAYED SO EAGERLY"

I prayed so eagerly,
"Turn and see
How bitter I have striven—
A word and all forgiven."
I prayed so eagerly.

I prayed so eagerly—
Not to be,
You turned and passed. Good-bye!
Fates smile for me, dreamed I—
Yet I prayed eagerly.

"WHEN THE DARK COMES"

When the dark comes,

"Is this the end?" I pray,
No answer from the night,
And then once more the day.
I take the world again
Upon my neck and go
Pace with the serious hours.
Since fate will have it so,
Begone dead man, unclasp
Your hands from round my heart,
I and my burden pass,
You and your peace depart.

DISTANT VOICES

I left my home for travelling;
Because I heard the strange birds sing
In foreign skies, and felt their wing

Brush past my soul impatiently;
I saw the bloom on flower and tree
That only grows beyond the sea.

Methought the distant voices spake
More wisdom than near tongues can make;
I followed—lest my heart should break.

And what is past is past and done.
I dreamt, and here the dream begun:
I saw a salmon in the sun

Leap from the river to the shore—
Ah! strange mishap, so wounded sore,
To his sweet stream to turn no more.

A bird from 'neath his mother's breast,
Spread his weak wings in vain request;
Never again to reach his nest.

I saw a blossom bloom too soon
Upon a summer's afternoon;
'Twill breathe no more beneath the moon.

I woke, warmed 'neath a foreign sky
Where locust blossoms bud and die,
Strange birds called to me flashing by.

And dusky faces passed and woke
The echoes with the words they spoke—
—The same old tales as other folk.

A truce to roaming! Never more
I'll leave the home I loved of yore.
But strangers meet me at the door.

I left my home still travelling,
For yet I hear the strange birds sing,
And foreign flowers rare perfumes bring.

I hear a distant voice, more wise
Than others are 'neath foreign skies.
I'll find—perhaps in paradise.

THE BALLAD OF THE FAIRY THORN-TREE

This is an evil night to go, my sister,
To the fairy-tree across the fairy rath,
Will you not wait till Hallow Eve is over?
For many are the dangers in your path!

I may not wait till Hallow Eve is over,
I shall be there before the night is fled,
For, brother, I am weary for my lover,
And I must see him once, alive or dead.

I've prayed to heaven, but it would not listen,
I'll call thrice in the devil's name to-night,
Be it a live man that shall come to hear me,
Or but a corpse, all clad in snowy white.

She had drawn on her silken hose and garter,
Her crimson petticoat was kilted high,
She trod her way amid the bog and brambles,
Until the fairy-tree she stood near-by.

When first she cried the devil's name so loudly
She listened, but she heard no sound at all;
When twice she cried, she thought from out the darkness
She heard the echo of a light footfall.

When last she cried her voice came in a whisper,
She trembled in her loneliness and fright;
Before her stood a shrouded, mighty figure,

In sombre garments blacker than the night.

"And if you be my own true love," she questioned,
"I fear you! Speak you quickly unto me."
"O, I am not your own true love," it answered,
"He drifts without a grave upon the sea."

"If he be dead, then gladly will I follow
Down the black stairs of death into the grave."
"Your lover calls you for a place to rest him
From the eternal tossing of the wave."

"I'll make my love a bed both wide and hollow,
A grave wherein we both may ever sleep."
"What give you for his body fair and slender,
To draw it from the dangers of the deep?"

"I'll give you both my silver comb and earrings,
I'll give you all my little treasure store."
"I will but take what living thing comes forward,
The first to meet you, passing to your door."

"O may my little dog be first to meet me,
So loose my lover from your dreaded hold."
"What will you give me for the heart that loved you,
The heart that I hold chained and frozen cold?"

"My own betrothed ring I give you gladly,
My ring of pearls—and every one a tear!"
"I will but have what other living creature
That second in your pathway shall appear."

"To buy this heart, to warm my love to living,
I pray my pony meet me on return."
"And now, for his young soul what will you give me,
His soul that night and day doth fret and burn?"

"You will not have my silver comb and earrings,
You will not have my ring of precious stone;
O, nothing have I left to promise to you,
But give my soul to buy him back his own."

All woefully she wept, and stepping homeward,
Bemoaned aloud her dark and cruel fate;
"O, come," she cried, "my little dog to meet me,
And you, my horse, be browsing at the gate."

Right hastily she pushed by bush and bramble,

Chased by a fear that made her footsteps fleet,
And as she ran she met her little brother,
Then her old father coming her to meet.

"O brother, little brother," cried she weeping,
"Well you said of fairy-tree beware,
For precious things are bought and sold ere mid-night,
On Hallow-eve, by those who barter there."

She went alone into the little chapel,
And knelt before the holy virgin's shrine,
Saying, "Mother Mary, pray you for me,
To save those two most gentle souls of thine."

And as she prayed, behold the holy statue
Spoke to her, saying, "Little can I aid,
God's ways are just, and you have dared to question
His judgment on this soul you bought—and paid."

"For that one soul, your father and your brother,
Your own immortal life you bartered; then,
Yet one chance is allowed—your sure repentance,
Give back his heart you made to live again."

"For these two souls—my father and my brother—
I give his heart back into death's cold land,
Never again to warm his dead, sweet body,
Or beat to madness underneath my hand."

"And for your soul—to save it from its sorrow,
You must drive back his soul into the night,
Back into righteous punishment and justice,
Or lose your chance of everlasting light."

"O, never shall I drive him back to anguish,
My soul shall suffer, letting his go free."
She rose, and weeping, left the little chapel,
Went forward blindly till she reached the sea.

She dug a grave within the surf and shingle,
A dark, cold bed, made very deep and wide,
She laid her down all stiff and stretched for burial,
Right in the pathway of the rising tide.

First tossed into her waiting arms the restless
Loud waves, a woman very grey and cold,
Within her bed she stood upright so quickly,
And loosed her fingers from the dead hands' hold.

The second who upon her heart had rested
From out the storm, a baby chill and stark,
With one long sob she drew it on her bosom,
Then thrust it out again into the dark.

The last who came so slow was her own lover,
She kissed his icy face on cheek and chin,
"O cold shall be your house to-night, beloved,
O cold the bed that we must sleep within.

"And heavy, heavy, on our lips so faithful
And on our hearts, shall lie our own roof-tree."
And as she spoke the bitter tears were falling
On his still face, all salter than the sea.

"And oh," she said, "if for a little moment
You knew, my cold, dead love, that I was by,
That my soul goes into the utter darkness
When yours comes forth—and mine goes in to die."

And as she wept she kissed his frozen forehead,
Laid her warm lips upon his mouth so chill,
With no response—and then the waters flowing
Into their grave, grew heavy, deep and still.

And so, 'tis said, if to that fairy thorn-tree
You dare to go, you see her ghost so lone,
She prays for love of her that you will aid her,
And give your soul to buy her back her own.

THE SUICIDE'S GRAVE

This is the scene of a man's despair, and a soul's release
From the difficult traits of the flesh; so, it seeking peace,
A shot rang out in the night; death's doors were wide;
And you stood alone, a stranger, and saw inside.

Coward flesh, brave soul, which was it? One feared the world,
The pity of men, or their scorn; yet carelessly hurled
All on the balance of Chance for a state unknown;
Fled the laughter of men for the anger of God—alone.

Perhaps when the hot blood streamed on the daisied sod,
Poor soul, you were likened to Cain, and you fled from God;
Men say you fought hard for your life, when the deed was done;

But your body would rise no more 'neath this world's sun.

I'd choose—should I do the act—such a night as this,
When the sea throws up white arms for the wild wind's kiss;
When the waves shake the shuddering shore with their foamy jaws;
Tear the strand, till slipping pebbles shriek through their claws.

The sky is loud with the storm; not a bird dare span
From here to the mist; beasts are silent; yet for a man,
For a soul springing naked to meet its judge, a night
That were as a brother to this poor spirit's long flight.

But he had chosen, they tell me, a dusk so fair
One almost thought there were not such another—there.
The air was full of the perfume of pines, and the sweet
Sleepy chirp of birds, long the lush soft grass at his feet.

They say there was dancing too in a house close by,
That they heard the shot just thinking wild birds must die.
They supped and laughed, went singing the long night through,
And they danced unknowing the dance of death with you.

What did you hear when you opened the doors of death?
Was it the sob of a thrush, or a slow sweet breath
Of the perfumed air that blew through the doors with you,
That you fought so hard to regain the world you knew?

Or was it a woman's cry that, shrieking into the gloom,
Like a hand that closed on your soul clutching it from its doom?
Was it a mother's call, or the touch of a baby's kiss,
That followed your desperate soul down the black abyss?

What did you see—as you stood on the other side—
A strange shy soul amongst souls, did you seek to hide
From the ghosts that were who judged you upon your way,
Reckoned your sins against theirs for the judgment day?

You feared the world, the pity of men or their scorn,
The movements of fate and the sorrows for which you were born.
Men's laughter, men's speech, their judging, what was it to this
Where the eyes of the dead proclaim you have done amiss.

Not peace did you gain, perhaps, nor the rest you had planned,
'Neath the horrible countless eyes that you could not withstand?
Or was it God looked from his throne in a moment's disdain,
And you shrieked for a trial once more in the height of your pain?

Perhaps—but who knows—when you struggled so hard for life's breath,

You saw nothing passing the grave except silence and death,
You lay shut in by the four clay walls of your cell,
There the live soul locked up in the stiff dead body's shell.

Dead, dead and coffin'd, buried beneath the clay,
And still the living soul caged in to wait decay,
For ever alone in night of unlifting gloom
There to think, and think, and think, in the silent tomb.

Or was it in death's cold land there was no perfume
Of the scented flowers, or lilt of a bird's gay tune.
No sea there, or no cool of a wind's fresh breath,
No woods, no plains, no dreams, and alas! no death?

Was there no life there that man's brain could understand?
No past, no future, hopes to come, in that strange land?
No human love, no sleep, no day, no night,
But ever eternal living in eternal light?

Perhaps the soul thus springing to fill its grave,
Found all the peace and happiness that it could crave;
All it had lost alone was that poor body's part
Which naught but grey corruption saw for its chart.

Ah well! for us there ended all one man's life with this—
A shot, a cry, a struggle, and a fainting woman's kiss;
Life's blood let 'mid the grasses—and all a world was lost,
And no one may ever know how he paid the cost.

He is lost in the crowd of the dead, in the night-time of death,
A name on a stone left to tell that he ever drew breath.
So desperate body die there, with your soul's long release,
And unhappy spirit God grant you Eternity's peace!

Dora Sigerson Shorter – A Concise Bibliography

Poetry Collections
Verses (1893)
The Fairy Changeling and Other Poems (1897)
The Collected Poems of Dora Sigerson Shorter (1907)
New Poems (1913)
The Sad Years (1918)
The Tricolour, Poems of the Irish Revolution (1922)

Novels
The Country-House Party (1905)

The Story and Song of Black Roderick (1906)
Through Wintry Terrors (1907)

Short Story collections
The Father Confessor, Stories of Death and Danger (1900)

www.ingramcontent.com/pod-product-compliance
Lightning Source LLC
Chambersburg PA
CBHW070110070426
42448CB00038B/2498